MORE OF JANICE VANCLEAVE'S
WILD, WACKY, AND WEIRD
BIOLOGY
EXPERIMENTS

Illustrations by
Lorna William

ROSEN
PUBLISHING

New York

This edition published in 2017 by
The Rosen Publishing Group, Inc.
29 East 21st Street
New York, NY 10010

Library of Congress Cataloging-in-Publication Data

Names: VanCleave, Janice.
Title: More of Janice VanCleave's wild, wacky, and weird biology experiments / Janice VanCleave.
Description: New York : Rosen YA, 2017. | Series: Janice Vancleave's wild, wacky, and weird science experiments | Includes index.
Identifiers: LCCN ISBN 9781499465419 (pbk.) | ISBN 9781499465433 (library bound) | ISBN 9781499465426 (6-pack)
Subjects: LCSH: Biology—Experiments—Juvenile literature.
Classification: LCC QH316.5 V364 2016 | DDC 570.78—dc23

Manufactured in the United States of America

Illustrations by Lorna William

Experiments first published in *Janice VanCleave's 202 Oozing, Bubbling, Dripping, and Bouncing Experiments* by John Wiley & Sons, Inc., copyright © 1996 Janice VanCleave, and *Janice VanCleave's 200 Gooey, Slippery, Slimy, Weird and Fun Experiments* by John Wiley & Sons, Inc., copyright © 1992 Janice VanCleave.

CONTENTS

INTRODUCTION

Biology is the study of the way living organisms behave and interact. Earth has been supporting the tiniest of single-celled living things for as many as 3.5 billion years. Arthropods, fish, plants, and mammals came later. Humans evolved about 200,000 years ago. The mysterious, ever-changing nature of living organisms makes it a popular branch of science to study.

The people who decide to work in the field of biology have a variety of career choices. Some biologists work outdoors in remote ecosystems. Other scientists work in laboratories to study topics as varied as cures for diseases, new marine species, or human DNA. Zoologists study animals, and botanists study plants. Most biologists study life on Earth, but astrobiologists search for life outside our planet. All these people have something in common: they are constantly asking questions to learn even more about living things.

This book is a collection of science experiments about biology. How does gravity affect plant growth? Can your mind turn sound into a mental picture? How does the brain get messages from the skin? You will find the answers to these and many other questions by doing the experiments in this book.

HOW TO USE THIS BOOK

You will be rewarded with successful experiments if you read each experiment carefully, follow the steps in order, and do not substitute materials. The following sections are included for all the experiments.

» **PURPOSE:** *The basic goals for the experiment.*

» **MATERIALS:** *A list of supplies you will need.*
You will experience less frustration and more fun if you gather all the necessary materials for the experiments before you begin. You lose your train of thought when you have to stop and search for supplies.

» **PROCEDURE:** *Step-by-step instructions on how to perform the experiment.* Follow each step very carefully, never skip steps, and do not add your own. Safety is of the utmost importance, and by reading the experiment before starting, then following the instructions exactly, you can feel confident that no unexpected results will occur. Ask an adult to help you when you are working with anything sharp or hot. If adult supervision is required, it will be noted in the experiment.

» **RESULTS:** *An explanation stating exactly what is expected to happen.* This is an immediate learning tool. If the expected results are achieved, you will know that you did the experiment correctly. If your results are not the same as described in the experiment, carefully read the instructions and start over from the first step.

» **WHY?** *An explanation of why the results were achieved.*

INTRODUCTION

THE SCIENTIFIC METHOD

Scientists identify a problem or observe an event. Then they seek solutions or explanations through research and experimentation. By doing the experiments in this book, you will learn to follow experimental steps and make observations. You will also learn many scientific principles that have to do with biology.

In the process, the things you see or learn may lead you to new questions. For example, perhaps you have completed the experiment that looks at the ability of the eye's pupil to change size. Now you wonder what would happen if you conducted the experiment while your subject wore sunglasses. That's great! All scientists are curious and ask new questions about what they learn. When you design a new experiment, it is a good idea to follow the scientific method.

1. Ask a question.

2. Do some research about your question. What do you already know?

3. Come up with a hypothesis, or a possible answer to your question.

4. Design an experiment to test your hypothesis. Make sure the experiment is repeatable.

5. Collect the data and make observations.

6. Analyze your results.

7. Reach a conclusion. Did your results support your hypothesis?

Many times, the experiment leads to more questions and a new experiment.

Always remember that when devising your own science experiment, have a knowledgeable adult review it with you before you try it out. Ask them to supervise it as well.

GROW A BEAN

PURPOSE To determine if the way seeds are planted affects the direction of root growth.

MATERIALS paper towels
clear drinking glass
masking tape
marking pen
4 pole bean seeds, such as Kentucky Wonder
tap water

PROCEDURE

1. Fold one paper towel and line the inside of the glass with it. Wad several paper towels and stuff them into the glass to hold the paper lining tightly against the glass.

2. Place a strip of tape around the outside of the glass.

3. On four sides of the glass, mark the tape with an arrow to indicate up, down, left, and right.

4. Place one bean seed between the glass and the paper towel lining under each arrow. Point the bean's concave side in the direction indicated by the arrow.

5. Moisten the paper towels in the glass with water. The paper should be moist, not dripping wet.

6. Keep the paper moist and observe for 5 to 7 days.

Note: Keep the glass of beans for the next experiment.

More of Janice VanCleave's Wild, Wacky, and Weird Biology Experiments

RESULTS No matter in which direction the bean is planted, the roots grow downward.

WHY? Plants contain auxin, a chemical that changes the speed of plant growth. Gravity causes the auxin to collect in the lower part of the plant. Root cells grow faster on the side where there is a smaller amount of auxin, causing this section to bend downward. The result is that auxin causes roots to grow down.

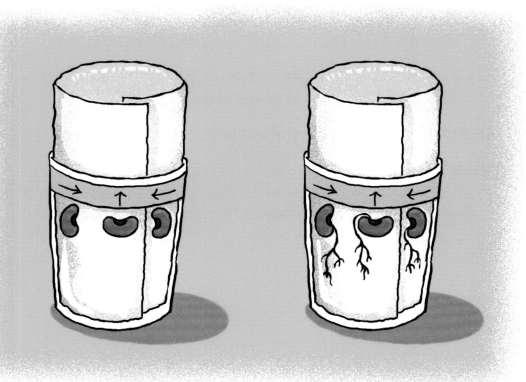

WINDERS

PURPOSE To determine the direction of winding plants.

MATERIALS masking tape
4 pencils
glass of growing beans from the previous experiment
tap water

PROCEDURE

1. Tape one pencil vertically to the outside of the glass in front of each plant. Have as much of the pencil as possible sticking up above the glass, so that the plant can wind around the pencil as it grows.

2. Allow the plant to stand for 2 weeks or longer. Be sure to keep the paper towel in the glass moist with water.

RESULTS The bean stems wind around the pencils.

WHY? The winding occurs because the part of the stem that is being touched does not grow as fast as the outside. As the outside of the stem increases in size, it forces the stem to wrap around whatever object it touches.

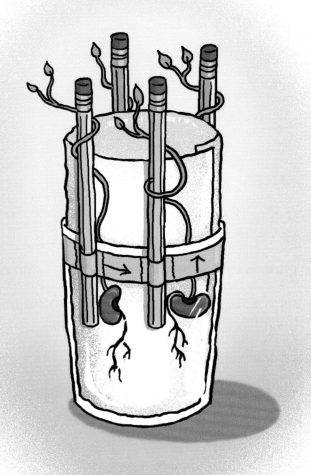

GROWTH RATE

PURPOSE To determine how shade affects growth in plants.

MATERIALS ruler
4 green onions
scissors
2 glasses
potting soil
tap water
pencil
adult helper

PROCEDURE

1. Measure about 6 inches (15 cm) from the root of each green onion and ask an adult to cut off the stems.

2. Fill the glasses with soil and moisten the soil with water.

3. In the soil of each glass, use the pencil to make two holes about 2 inches (5 cm) deep near the side of the glass.

4. Plant one onion in each hole.

5. Place one glass near a window so that it receives sunlight and place the other glass in a shady part of the room.

6. Each day for 14 days, mark each stem just above the outer skin covering, as shown in the diagram.

RESULTS The leaves on the onions placed in the shade are longer than those placed in the sun.

WHY? The lack of sunlight triggers growth in the onion as in all plants. This growth increases a plant's chances of growing out from under the shade. If the plant does not reach sufficient sunlight, however, it will eventually die.

FLOWER MAZE

PURPOSE To demonstrate that plants grow toward light.

MATERIALS paper cup
potting soil
3 pinto beans
tap water
scissors
cardboard
shoe box with a lid
masking tape

PROCEDURE

1. Fill the cup with soil and plant the beans in the soil.

2. Moisten the soil and allow the beans to sprout (about 5 to 7 days).

3. Cut two cardboard pieces to fit vertically inside the shoe box.

4. Secure the cardboard with tape to form a maze, as shown in the diagram.

5. Cut a hole at one end of the lid.

6. Place the bean plant inside the shoe box at one end.

7. Secure the box lid with the hole on the opposite end from the plant.

8. Open the lid daily to observe the plant's growth. Water the soil when needed.

9. Continue to observe until the plant grows out the hole in the lid.

RESULTS The plant winds around the obstacles and out the hole in the lid.

WHY? The plant grows toward the light. This growth of a plant in response to light is called phototropism. A buildup of auxin occurs on the dark side of the stem. Auxin causes stem cells to grow longer on the dark side, which forces the stem to bend toward light.

GROWING SEASON

PURPOSE To demonstrate the effect of temperature on seed growth.

MATERIALS 2 drinking glasses
paper towels
8 pinto beans
tap water

PROCEDURE

1. Prepare both glasses as follows:

a. Fold one paper towel and line the inside of the glass with it.

b. Wad several paper towels and stuff them into the glass to hold the paper lining against the glass.

c. Place four beans between the glass and the paper towel lining. Evenly space the beans around the center of the glass.

2. Moisten the paper towels in the glasses with water. The paper should be moist but not dripping wet.

3. Place one glass in the refrigerator and keep the other at normal room temperature.

4. Keep the paper in both glasses moist and observe for 7 or more days.

RESULTS The beans at room temperature have started to grow, but the ones in the refrigerator are unchanged.

WHY? Seeds need a specific temperature to grow, and pinto beans require warmth. Very few seeds sprout during the colder months. Most are dormant (inactive) during the cold parts of the year and start to grow when the ground warms.

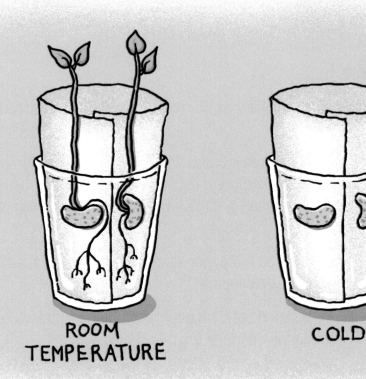

ROOM
TEMPERATURE

COLD

Pictures from Sound

PURPOSE To show that the mind can change sound messages into mental pictures.

MATERIALS scissors
poster board
2 plastic or cardboard school/pencil boxes
marking pen
masking tape
2 marbles
helper

PROCEDURE

1. Without your helper seeing their contents, prepare two boxes as follows.

2. Cut two strips from the poster board. One must fit diagonally across the inside of a box and the other must fit perpendicularly across the inside of a box. Be sure the lid of the box will close when these strips are in position.

3. Label one box 1 and tape the paper strip diagonally across. Add one marble and tape the box closed.

4. Label the other box 2 and tape the paper strip perpendicularly across the box. Add one marble and tape the box closed.

5. Ask your helper to rotate each box back and forth and determine the shape of the open space inside each box from the sounds heard.

RESULTS The sound of the rolling marble allows your helper to determine the inside structure of each box.

WHY? As the marble moves around, your helper makes mental notes about the length of time before the marble hits something. When enough information is put together, your helper can form a mental picture of the inside of each box.

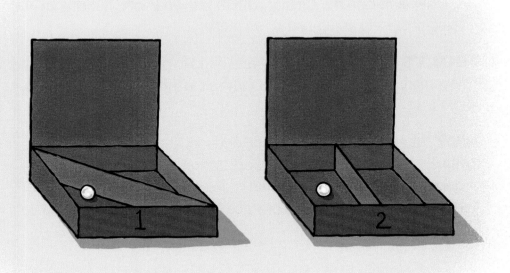

CONCENTRATION

PURPOSE To test your power of concentration.

MATERIALS chair

PROCEDURE

1. Sit in the chair with your feet on the floor.

2. Use your right foot to trace a clockwise pattern on the floor.

3. Keep your foot going in a circle while you move your right hand around in a clockwise pattern in front of your body.

4. Continue tracing the circular pattern with your foot, but change the hand pattern to an up-and-down motion.

RESULTS It is easy for the foot and hand to perform the same pattern of movement, but difficult to move them simultaneously in two different patterns.

WHY? When the patterns for hand and foot are the same, repetitive movement is easy. Up-and-down or circular patterns are easily done, but only when one pattern at a time is being processed by the brain. It takes much concentration and practice to successfully accomplish both patterns simultaneously.

Concentration

IN THE WAY

PURPOSE To demonstrate the body's automatic balance responses.

MATERIALS wall

PROCEDURE

1. Stand with your feet about 12 inches (30 cm) apart, and with your right foot and right shoulder against the wall.

2. Try to bend your left knee so that your left foot is lifted about 4 inches (10 cm) above the floor.

RESULTS You start to fall over when you raise your foot.

WHY? Raising the left foot causes the body's center of gravity to extend past the body's supportive foundation—the foot on the floor. The body automatically leans slightly to the right to redistribute the body's weight and again place its center of gravity over the supportive foot. When standing next to the wall, the body is prevented from leaning to the right, so you cannot balance with your foot raised.

In the Way

BLINKING

PURPOSE To determine if blinking is an involuntary action.

MATERIALS helper
glasses or lightly tinted sunglasses
cotton ball

NOTE: If sunglasses are used, they must be lightly tinted so that you can easily see your helper's eyes through them.

PROCEDURE

CAUTION: Do not substitute materials without adult approval. It could be dangerous to throw anything other than a cotton ball.

1. Have your helper wear his or her glasses.

2. Stand about 1 yard (1 m) away from your helper.

3. Without letting your helper know it is coming, throw a cotton ball directly at your helper's face. The glasses will keep the cotton ball from hitting your helper in the eyes.

RESULTS Your helper will blink, and possibly jerk or raise a hand, to protect his or her eyes.

WHY? The sudden unexpected approach of the cotton ball causes your helper's eyes to blink. Blinking is a reflex action. Like other reflex actions, it is not controlled by thinking about it. The involuntary movement of the eyelids, head, and hand happens because nerve cells in the eyes send messages to nerve cells in the brain and spinal cord. The instructions are then quickly passed on to the muscles, resulting in the protective movements of blinking, jerking the head, and raising the hand in front of the face.

NUMB

PURPOSE To demonstrate how the brain interprets messages from sensory receptors in the skin.

MATERIALS pencil

PROCEDURE

1. Use the index finger and thumb of your right hand to rub the upper- and undersides of the index finger of your left hand.

2. Hold the pencil in your left hand against the underside of the index finger on that hand.

3. Use your right thumb and index finger to rub the upper side of your left index finger and the pencil at the same time.

RESULTS When the pencil is held against the finger and both are rubbed, it feels as if part of your finger is numb.

WHY? When you rub your finger, mechanoreceptors (cells that are stimulated by pressure, touch, or sound) on both sides of the touched finger send messages to the brain. Mechanoreceptors on the finger and thumb of the hand doing the rubbing are also sending messages. These messages are analyzed by the brain, which sends an output message that results in the sensation that you are rubbing both sides of your finger. When the pencil is rubbed instead of the finger's underside, a message is missing. The brain interprets the missing information to mean that the finger is numb on one side. The brain takes in and puts out information based on what the sensory receptors tell it. Even though you know better, the output message is that your finger is numb.

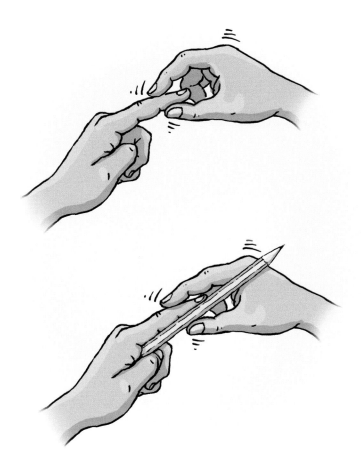

Open and Close

PURPOSE To demonstrate the ability of the eye's pupil to change size.

MATERIALS penlight
helper

PROCEDURE

1. Ask your helper to sit in a very dimly lighted room with both eyes open.

2. After 2 to 3 minutes, observe the size of the pupils in both eyes.

3. Hold the penlight close to, but not touching, the side of your helper's face. Slowly move the penlight so that the beam of light moves across the side of the face and shines directly into the pupil of one eye. Immediately turn off the penlight.

CAUTION: Do not shine the light into your helper's eye for more than 1 second.

4. Repeat the previous step with the opposite eye.

5. Compare the size of the pupils before and after shining the light into the eyes.

RESULTS The pupils are much larger before shining a light into the eyes.

WHY? The iris (colored muscular circle in the front of the eye) controls the amount of light entering the eye by making the dotlike opening in its center, the pupil, larger or smaller. In dim light, the pupil dilates (gets bigger), allowing more light to enter the eye. In bright light, the pupil contracts (gets smaller) to protect the inside of the eye from excessive light.

MUSCLE POWER

PURPOSE To locate the muscle pair in the upper arm.

MATERIALS chair
helper

PROCEDURE

1. Ask your helper to sit in the chair next to a heavy table.

2. Instruct your helper to place one hand, palm up, under the table's edge and push up carefully with medium pressure.

3. While pressure is being applied to the table, feel the front and back of your helper's upper arm.

4. Next, ask your helper to place his or her hand, palm down, on top of the table and press down.

5. Again, feel the same parts of your helper's upper arm.

RESULTS When the hand is pushing up on the table, the muscle in the front feels harder than the muscle in the back of the arm. When the hand is pressing down on the table, the muscle in the back of the arm feels harder.

WHY? Even though the joint (place where bones meet) in the arm—the elbow—is not being bent and straightened, the muscle pair in the upper arm that causes these movements is identified in this activity. Pushing up on the table causes the flexor muscle (muscle that bends a joint) in the front of the arm to contract and harden. Pushing down on the table causes the extensor muscle (muscle that straightens a joint) in the back of the arm to contract and harden.

STRONGER

PURPOSE To determine how sniffing affects the intensity of smells.

MATERIALS vanilla extract
2 cotton balls
baby food jar
timer

PROCEDURE

1. Place a few drops of the vanilla on one of the cotton balls.

2. Drop the moistened cotton ball into the jar.

3. Hold the opening of the jar under, but not touching, your nose.

4. Breathe normally for one or two breaths and note the strength of the smell of the vanilla.

5. Discard the cotton ball in the jar.

6. Wait 5 minutes, then repeat steps 1 and 2 with the other cotton ball, again holding the opening of the jar under, but not touching, your nose.

7. Take a good sniff by inhaling deeply.

RESULTS The smell of the vanilla is stronger when you take a good sniff than when you breathe normally.

WHY? In normal breathing, some of the air carrying the vanilla molecules (smallest particles of a substance) fills the nasal cavity but most of the air passes through the nasal cavity and into the back of the throat. When you take a good sniff, currents of air are drawn upward, flowing over the chemoreceptors (cells that are stimulated by smell or taste) located high up at the back of your nose. Sniffing also brings in more air containing the vanilla molecules.

HOT OR COLD?

PURPOSE To demonstrate that sensations of cold or hot can be deceiving.

MATERIALS three 2-quart (2-liter) bowls
cold and warm tap water
5 ice cubes
spoon
thermometer

PROCEDURE

1. Fill two of the bowls three-fourths full with cold tap water. Allow one bowl to stand for 5 minutes to reach room temperature. This will be the medium water.

2. Add the ice cubes to the second bowl. Stir until the ice cubes are about half melted. This will be the cold water.

3. Fill the third bowl three-fourths full with warm tap water. This will be the warm water. Use the thermometer to make sure it is about 113 degrees Fahrenheit (45°C).

CAUTION: If hotter, add cold water, stir, and check the temperature before proceeding.

4. Place the bowls on a table with the cold water on your right, the medium water in the middle, and the warm water on your left.

5. Put your right hand in the cold water and your left hand in the warm water. After 20 seconds, remove your hands from the outer bowls and put both hands in the center bowl.

RESULTS The same water feels warm to your right hand but cold to your left hand.

WHY? Heat tends to flow from an object with a higher temperature to an object with a lower temperature. The medium water feels warm to your right hand because it had been soaking in icy water. The heat energy flowed from the warm water to your cold skin. The skin of your left hand was warmer than the medium water. Thus, the energy flowed away from the skin, making the medium water feel cold to your left hand.

COLD   MEDIUM   WARM

GRIPPER

PURPOSE To determine how the ridges on fingertips affect the ability to pick up objects.

MATERIALS dishwashing gloves
assortment of small coins

PROCEDURE

1. Put one glove on the hand you write with.

2. Spread the coins out on a table.

3. Pick up each coin one at a time with the hand covered with the rubber glove. Place each coin back on the table before lifting the next coin.

4. Make note of the ease or difficulty in lifting each coin from the table.

5. Note the texture of the fingers of the gloves.

6. Remove the glove from your hand.

7. Turn the glove that does not fit your writing hand inside out.

8. Put the inside-out glove on your writing hand.

9. Again, pick each coin up one at a time with the hand covered with the rubber glove. Place each coin back on the table before lifting the next coin.

10. Make note of the ease or difficulty in lifting each coin from the table's surface.

11. Again, note the texture of the fingers of the glove.

RESULTS The coins are easily picked up when the glove is right side out, but are difficult or impossible to pick up when the glove is inside out.

WHY? The fingertips are rough when the glove is on properly and smooth when the glove is inside out. The textured tips of the glove act like the ridged skin on the tips of your fingers, which cause fingerprints. The ridges in the rubber, as well as in your skin, increase friction and allow you to pick up objects more easily. Friction is the resistance to motion between two surfaces that are touching each other. Without the ridges on your fingertips, your fingers would tend to slide over objects, making it difficult to pick them up, just as it was difficult with the smooth tips of the inside-out glove.

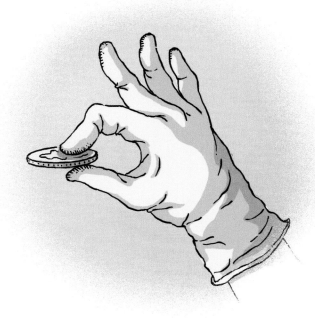

HUMMING

PURPOSE To determine how you make sounds.

PROCEDURE

1. Hum a tune with your mouth open.

2. Continue to hum, but close your mouth.

3. Pinch your nose closed with your fingers and hum with your mouth open.

4. Close your mouth, hum a tune, and pinch your nose closed again.

RESULTS You can hum as long as your mouth and/or your nose is open, but if both are closed, you cannot hum.

WHY? When you hum or make any other sounds, air passes between the vocal cords in your throat and causes them to vibrate. When your mouth and nose are closed, the air flow stops. Thus, the vibrations stop and the sound stops along with them.

SPICY ESCAPE

PURPOSE To demonstrate diffusion and osmosis.

MATERIALS eyedropper
vanilla extract
small balloon
shoe box

PROCEDURE

1. Use the eyedropped to put 15 drops of vanilla extract inside the deflated balloon. Be careful not to get any of the vanilla on the outside of the balloon.

2. Inflate the balloon to a size that will comfortably fit inside the shoe box and tie the open end.

3. Place the balloon in the empty shoe box. Leave the balloon in the closed box for 1 hour.

4. Open the box and smell the air inside.

RESULTS The air smells like vanilla. The box is still dry.

WHY? The balloon appears to be solid, but it actually has very small invisible holes all over its surface. The liquid vanilla molecules are too large to pass through the holes, but the molecules of vanilla vapor are smaller than the holes and pass through. The movement of the vapor through the rubber membrane is called diffusion.

FLUFFY RAISINS

PURPOSE To observe the effect of osmosis on a raisin.

MATERIALS glass of water
10 to 12 raisins

PROCEDURE

1. Place the raisins in the glass of water.

2. Allow them to stand overnight.

RESULTS The raisins swell, and become fluffy and smooth.

WHY? During osmosis, water moves from a greater concentration through a membrane to an area of lesser water concentration. The raisins were dry inside, thus the water in the glass moved through the cell membranes into the raisins. As the cells filled with water, the raisins became plump and fluffy.

STAND UP

PURPOSE To demonstrate how the change in turgor pressure causes plant stems to wilt.

MATERIALS wilted stalk of celery
1 drinking glass
blue food coloring

PROCEDURE

1. Ask an adult to cut a slice from the bottom of a wilted celery stalk.

2. Put enough food coloring into a glass half full of water to turn it dark blue.

3. Allow the celery to stand overnight in the blue water.

RESULTS The celery leaves become a blue-green color, and the stalk is firm and crisp.

WHY? A fresh cut across the bottom ensures that the celery cells are not closed off or dried out. Water enters into the water-conducting tubes called xylem. These tubes run the length of the stalk of the celery. Water leaves the xylem tubes and enters the cells up and down the celery stalk. Plants usually stand erect and return to their original position when gently bent. This happens because each plant cell is normally full of water. The water makes each cell firm, and all the cells together cause the plant to be rigid. A plant wilts when it is deprived of water, and like half-filled balloons, the cells collapse, causing leaves and stems to droop. The pressure of the water inside the plant cell is called turgor pressure.

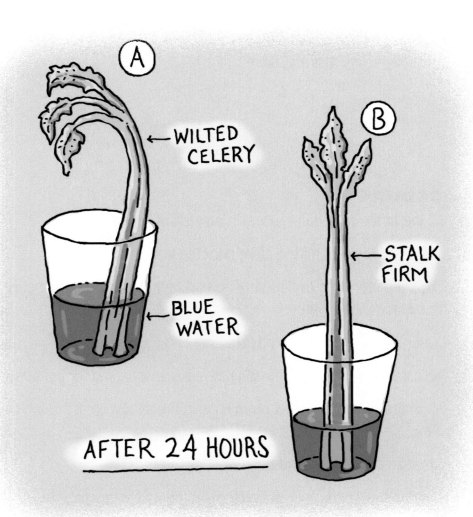

A

← WILTED CELERY

BLUE WATER →

B

← STALK FIRM

AFTER 24 HOURS

LEAF STRAW

PURPOSE To demonstrate that the leaves and stems of plants can act like a straw.

MATERIALS glass soda bottle
ivy leaf and stem
clay
pencil
straw
mirror

PROCEDURE

1. Fill the bottle with water to within an inch of its top.

2. Wrap the clay around the stem near the leaf.

3. Place the stem into the bottle. The end of the stem must be below the surface of the water.

4. Cover the mouth of the bottle with the clay.

5. Push the pencil through the clay to make an opening for the straw.

6. Insert the straw so that its opening is in the air space at the top of the bottle.

7. Squeeze the clay around the straw.

8. Stand in front of the mirror and look at the mirror image of the bottle while you suck the air out of the bottle through the straw. This should be difficult if there are no leaks in the clay, so use a lot of suction.

RESULTS Bubbles start forming at the bottom of the stem.

WHY? There are holes in the leaf called stomata, and tiny tubes called xylem run down the stem. The leaf and stem acted like a straw. As you sucked air out of the straw, more was drawn in through the leaf straw. It is through these tubes and holes that water moves in a plant.

WHAT ARE STOMATA?

PURPOSE To determine which side of the plant leaf takes in gases.

MATERIALS potted plant
petroleum jelly

PROCEDURE

1. Coat the top of four leaves with a heavy layer of petroleum jelly.

2. Coat the underside of another four leaves with a heavy layer of petroleum jelly.

3. Observe the leaves daily for 1 week.

4. Is there any difference in the two sets of leaves?

RESULTS The leaves that had petroleum jelly coated on the underside died. The other leaves remained unchanged.

WHY? Openings on the underside of plant leaves called stomata allow gases to move into and out of the leaves. The petroleum jelly plugged the openings and the leaf was not able to receive necessary carbon dioxide gas or eliminate excess oxygen gas.

What Are Stomata?

WATER LOSS

PURPOSE To demonstrate transpiration, the loss of water from leaves.

MATERIALS leafy plant
plastic sandwich bag
transparent tape

PROCEDURE

1. Place the sandwich bag over one leaf.

2. Secure the bag to the stem with the tape.

3. Place the plant in sunlight for 2 to 3 hours.

4. Observe the inside of the bag.

RESULTS Droplets of water collect on the inside of the plastic bag. The inside of the bag may appear cloudy due to the water in the air.

WHY? Plants absorb water from the soil through their roots. This water moves up the stem to the leaves, where 90 percent is lost through the pores of the leaf (stomata). Some trees lose as much as 15,000 pounds (6,818 kg) of water within a 12-hour period. Plants can greatly affect the temperature and humidity of a heavily vegetated area. This loss of water through the stomata of the leaves is called transpiration.

INDEPENDENCE

PURPOSE To demonstrate the independence of plants.

MATERIALS 1 gallon (4 L) jar with a large mouth and lid
small potted plant

PROCEDURE

1. Moisten the soil of the plant.

2. Place the entire plant, pot and all, inside the gallon jar.

3. Close the jar with its lid.

4. Place the jar somewhere that receives sunlight for part of the day.

5. Leave the jar closed for 30 days.

RESULTS Periodically, drops of water will be seen on the inside of the jar. The plant continues to grow.

WHY? The water drops come from the moisture in the soil and from the plant leaves. Plants use the sugar in their cells plus oxygen from the air to produce carbon dioxide, water, and energy. This is called the respiration reaction. They can use the carbon dioxide, water, chlorophyll, and light energy in their cells to produce sugar and oxygen. This process is called photosynthesis. Notice that the products of the respiration reaction fuel the photosynthesis reaction and vice versa. Plants continue to make their own food. They eventually die in the closed bottle because the nutrients in the soil are used up.

WATER DROPS

UP OR DOWN?

PURPOSE To observe the effects of gravity on plant growth.

MATERIALS houseplant
books

PROCEDURE

1. Lay the pot on its side on the books.

2. Observe the position of the stem and leaves for 1 week.

RESULTS The stem and leaves turn upward.

WHY? Plants contain a chemical called auxin. Auxin causes plant cells to grow extra long. Gravity pulls the plant chemical downward so that along the bottom of the stem there is a buildup of auxin. The cells grow longer where the auxin buildup is, causing the stem to turn upward.

Up or Down?

GLOSSARY

AUXIN A chemical that changes the speed of plant growth.

CENTER OF GRAVITY Point at which an object balances.

CHEMORECEPTOR A sensory receptor that is stimulated by smell or taste.

CONTRACT To get smaller.

DIFFUSION The mixing of molecules because of molecular motion.

DILATE To get bigger.

DORMANT Inactive.

EXTENSOR MUSCLE A muscle that straightens a joint.

FLEXOR MUSCLE A muscle that bends a joint.

FRICTION The resistance of motion between two surfaces that are touching each other.

GRAVITY Force that pulls toward the center of a celestial body, such as the earth.

MECHANORECEPTORS Cells that are stimulated by pressure, touch, or sound.

OSMOSIS The movement of water through a semipermeable membrane; movement is toward the side with the least water concentration.

PHOTOTROPISM Plant growth in response to light.

SPINAL CORD The large bundle of nerves that runs through the discs of the spine.

STOMATA Very small openings on a leaf through which gases are exchanged.

TRANSPIRATION The passing of water, in plants, from the roots through the plant and into the air.

VIBRATE To move quickly back and forth.

XYLEM Tiny tubes in the stalk of a plant that run through the leaves and stems; they transport water and food to the plant's cells.

FOR MORE INFORMATION

The National Geographic Society
  1145 17th Street NW
  Washington, DC 20036
  (202) 857-7700
  website: http://www.nationalgeographic.com
  The National Geographic Society has been inspiring people to care about the planet since 1888. It is one of the largest nonprofit scientific and educational institutions in the world. Read their Kids magazine, enter the National Geographic Bee, or visit the museum.

National Science Foundation (NSF)
  4201 Wilson Boulevard
  Arlington, VA 22230
  (703) 292-5111
  website: http://www.nsf.gov
  The NSF is dedicated to science, engineering, and education. Learn how to be a citizen scientist, read about the latest scientific discoveries, and discover the newest innovations in technology.

The National Zoological Park
  3001 Connecticut Avenue NW
  Washington, DC 20008
  (202) 633-4888
  website: http://nationalzoo.si.edu
  The National Zoological Park is a part of the Smithsonian Institution, the world's largest museum and research complex. Join a nature camp, watch the newest arrivals at the zoo through their live-streaming animal webcams, or learn more about wildlife research expeditions.

Royal Botanical Gardens
  680 Plains Road West
  Burlington, ON
  Canada
  (800) 694-4769
  website: http://www.rbg.ca
  The Royal Botanical Gardens is the largest botanical garden in Canada, a National Historic Site, and a registered charitable organization with the goal of bringing together people, plants, and nature.

The Society for Science and the Public
  Student Science
  1719 N Street NW
  Washington, DC 20036
  (800) 552-4412
  website: http://student.societyforscience.org
  The Society for Science and the Public presents many science resources, such as science news for students, the latest updates on the Intel Science Talent Search and the Intel International Science and Engineering Fair, and information about cool jobs in science.

WEBSITES

Due to the changing nature of internet links, Rosen Publishing has developed an online list of websites related to the subject of this book. This site is updated regularly. Please use this link to access this list:

http://www.rosenlinks.com/JVCW/bio

FOR FURTHER READING

Ardley, Neil. *101 Great Science Experiments.* New York, NY: DK Ltd., 2014.

Barnes-Svarney, Patricia L. *The Handy Anatomy Answer Book* (The Handy Answer Book Series). Detroit, MI: Visible Ink Press, 2016.

Buczynski, Sandy. *Designing a Winning Science Fair Project* (Information Explorer Junior). Ann Arbor, MI: Cherry Lake Publishing, 2014.

Butterfield, Moira. *The Human Body* (Know It All). New York, NY: Cavendish Square, 2016.

Dickmann, Nancy. *Life Cycles* (Earth Figured Out). New York, NY: Cavendish Square, 2016.

Franchino, Vicky. *Animal Camouflage* (True Book). New York, NY: Children's Press, 2016.

Goldish, Meish. *Inside the Worm's Hole* (Snug As a Bug: Where Bugs Live). New York, NY: Bearport Publishing, 2014.

Gray, Leon. *Amazing Animal Engineers* (Fact Finders: Animal Scientists). North Mankato, MN: Capstone Press, 2016.

Hawkins, Jay. *It's Alive! The Science of Plants and Living Things* (Big Bang Science Experiments). New York, NY: Windmill Books, 2013.

Latham, Donna. *Backyard Biology: Investigate Habitats Outside Your Door with 25 Projects* (Build It Yourself). White River Junction, VT: Nomad Press, 2013.

Lawrence, Ellen. *Dirt* (Fundamental Experiments). New York, NY: Bearport Publishing, 2013.

Lawrence, Ellen. *Why Do Most Plants Need Soil?* (Down & Dirty: The Secrets of Soil). New York, NY: Bearport Publishing, 2016.

Meister, Cari. *Totally Wacky Facts About the Human Body* (Mind Benders). North Mankato, MN: Capstone, 2016.

Rocket, Paul. *100 Trillion Good Bacteria Living on the Human Body* (Big Countdown). Chicago, IL: Capstone Raintree, 2016.

INDEX

phototropism, 15
plants
    growth of, 12, 14, 15, 16–17, 52,
        54
    leaves, 46–47, 50
    roots, 9, 12
    seeds, 8, 16, 17
    stems, 10, 12, 15, 44, 46–47, 48,
        50, 54
    wilting, 44

R
reflex, 25
respiration reaction, 52

S
safety, 5, 7
scientific method, 6–7
sensory receptors, 26–27
sound, 18–19
spinal cord, 25
stomata, 47, 48, 50
sunlight, 12, 13, 15, 50, 52

T
temperature, 16–17, 34–35, 50
transpiration, 50
turgor pressure, 44

V
vocal cords, 38

X
xylem, 44

Z
zoologists, 4